NATIVE AMERICAN SPIRIT BEINGS

NATIVE AMERICAN SPIRIT BEINGS

EDITED BY JEANNE NAGLE

Educational Publishing

IN ASSOCIATION WITH

EDUCATIONAL SERVICES

Published in 2015 by Britannica Educational Publishing (a trademark of Encyclopædia Britannica, Inc.) in association with The Rosen Publishing Group, Inc. 29 East 21st Street, New York, NY 10010

Distributed exclusively by Rosen Publishing.

To see additional Britannica Educational Publishing titles, go to http://www.rosenpublishing.com

First Edition

Britannica Educational Publishing
J.E. Luebering: Director, Core Reference Group
Anthony L. Green: Editor, Compton's by Britannica

Rosen Publishing
Hope Lourie Killcoyne: Executive Editor
Jeanne Nagle: Editor
Nelson Sá: Art Director
Nicole Russo: Designer
Cindy Reiman: Photography Manager
Marty Levick: Photo Researcher
Additional material by Kathleen Kuiper

Cataloging-in-Publication Data

Native American spirit beings/[edited by] Jeanne Nagle.—First Edition.
        pages cm.—(Gods and goddesses of mythology)
Includes bibliographical references and index.
ISBN 978-1-62275-399-4 (library bound)
1. Indian mythology—North America—Juvenile literature.
2. Indians of North America—Religion—Juvenile literature.
I. Nagle, Jeanne.
E98.R3N38 2015
299.7—dc23

2013051224

Manufactured in the United States of America

On the cover: Native American totem poles in Vancouver, British Columbia, Canada.
Adina Tovy/Lonely Planet Images/Getty Images

Interior pages graphic © *iStockphoto.com/Radiocat*

CONTENTS

Artist Severino Baraldi's interpretation of a Sioux ghost dance. Private
Collection/© Look and Learn/ The Bridgeman Art Library

U ntil the 1950s it was commonly assumed that the religions of the surviving Native Americans were little more than curious anachronisms, dying remnants of humankind's childhood. These traditions lacked sacred texts and fixed doctrines or moral codes and were embedded in societies without wealth, mostly without writing, and without recognizable systems of politics or justice or any of the usual indicators of civilization. Today the situation has changed dramatically. Scholars of religion, students of the ecological sciences, and individuals committed to expanding and deepening their own religious lives have found in these traditions many distinct and varied religious worlds that have struggled to survive but that retain the ability to inspire.

The histories of these worlds are also marked by loss. Five hundred years of political, economic, and religious domination have taken their toll. Scholars note when complex ceremonies become extinct, but often community members mourn even more the disappearance of small daily rituals and of religious vocabularies and

9

grammars embedded in traditional languages—an erosion of memories that include not only formal sacred narratives but the myriad informal strands that once composed these tightly woven ways of life. Nevertheless, despite the pervasive effects of modern society, from which there is no longer any possibility of geographic, economic, or technological isolation, there are instances of remarkable continuity with the past, as well as remarkably creative adaptation to the present and anticipation of the future.

Native American people themselves often claim that their traditional ways of life do not include "religion." They find the term difficult, often impossible, to translate into their own languages. This apparent incongruity arises from differences in cosmology and epistemology. Western tradition distinguishes religious thought and action as that whose ultimate authority is supernatural—which is to say, beyond, above, or outside both phenomenal nature and human reason. In most indigenous worldviews there is no such antithesis. Plants and animals, clouds and mountains carry and embody revelation. Even where native tradition conceives of a realm or world apart from the terrestrial one and not normally visible from it, as in the case of the Iroquois Sky World or the several underworlds of Pueblo cosmologies, the boundaries between these worlds are permeable. The ontological distance between land and sky or between land and underworld is short and is traversed in both directions.

Instead of encompassing a duality of sacred and profane, indigenous religious traditions seem to conceive only of sacred and more sacred. Spirit, power, or something akin moves in all things, though not equally. For native communities religion is understood as the relationship between living humans and other persons or things, however they are conceived. These may include departed as well as yet-to-be-born human beings, beings in the so-called "natural world" of flora and fauna, and visible entities that are not animate by Western standards, such as mountains, springs, lakes, and clouds. This group of entities also includes what scholars of religion might denote as "mythic beings," beings that are not normally visible but are understood to inhabit and affect either this world or some other world contiguous to it.

Because religions of this kind are so highly localized, it is impossible to determine exactly how many exist in North America now or may have existed in the past. Distinct languages in North America at the time of the first European contact are often estimated in the vicinity of 300, which linguists have variously grouped into some 30 to 50 families. Consequently, there is great diversity among these traditions. For instance, Iroquois longhouse elders speak frequently about the Creator's "Original Instructions" to human beings, using male gender references and attributing to this divinity not only the planning and organizing of creation but qualities of goodness, wisdom, and perfection that are reminiscent of the Christian deity. By contrast, the Koyukon universe is notably decentralized. Raven, whom Koyukon narratives credit with the creation of human beings, is only one among many powerful entities in the Koyukon world. He exhibits human weaknesses such as lust and pride, is neither all-knowing nor all-good, and teaches more often by counterexample than by his wisdom.

A similarly sharp contrast is found in Navajo and Pueblo ritual. Most traditional Navajo ceremonies are enacted on behalf of individuals in response to specific needs. Most Pueblo ceremonial work is communal, both in participation and in perceived benefit, and is scheduled according to natural cycles. Still, the healing benefits of a Navajo sing naturally spread through the families of all those participating, while the communal benefits of Pueblo ceremonial work naturally redound to individuals.

Thus, there is no such thing as a generic "Native American religion." Attempts to understand these religious traditions en masse are bound to produce oversimplification and distortion. Instead, it may be useful to consider the broad characteristics that pertain to the religious lives of many indigenous North American communities.

In the Native American experience, place is important, and religious practices are often localized. The importance of place is revealed in the beliefs of the Menominee, who use local geography to explain the origin of their people, and the Iroquois, whose longhouses are understood as microcosms of the universe. Moreover, traditional knowledge, passed on orally across the generations, maintains the memory of visible and invisible inhabitants of a place. Access to some kinds of knowledge, however, is restricted. Actions, words, and thoughts are understood in many traditions to have power in the world. Some knowledge may be considered so powerful and dangerous that a process of instruction and initiation is required for those who will use it.

Participation is more important than belief. Arguments about doctrinal truth are largely absent from most native North American religious traditions. Good-hearted participation in the ceremonial and everyday work of the community is the main requirement. However, knowledgeable people with considerable life experience may discuss such matters informally.

Cooperation with and devotion to the larger kin group is a central part of small-scale societies, and this is true of Native American communities. Teaching proper behaviour toward others, which is defined by one's relationship to them, is an essential part of child rearing. This instruction is religious as well because of the expectation that the entire world, one's life, and one's other-than-human relatives will be treated in the same way as all human relatives.

Generosity, in the Native American tradition, is a religious act as well as a social one. The value of generosity is perhaps most dramatically figured in the northern practice known in English as giveaway or in the potlatch of the Northwest Coast peoples, in which property and gifts are ceremonially distributed. Human beings are taught to give eagerly because in so doing they imitate the generosity of the many other-than-human entities that provide for human sustenance.

A community's oral narratives contain a record of human interaction with other-than-human beings, powers, and entities in a place. In addition to the more solemn genres, such as creation stories and migration narratives, there are moralistic stories, family histories, instruction meant to teach traditional skills, and many kinds of jokes. Moreover, joking, clowning, and other forms of entertainment are integral parts of many ceremonial events and settings, either formally or informally. Sometimes such performances are a means of shaming individuals into correcting troublesome behaviour, but they are also employed simply to spread happiness and to lighten moods.

Significant achievements and life passages are meant to be shared by relatives and the community. Various forms of coming-of-age and initiation ceremonies make up a large portion of the ritual repertoire of many Native American traditions. These ceremonies provide structures for instruction in traditional knowledge, but, more important, they reintegrate an individual into kin, community, and cosmos when new status is attained.

One of the more important life passages is death, which is understood as a transition and not an ending.

13

Beliefs about death, and ritual responses to it, however, are among the more heterogeneous aspects of Native American religious life. Many Native American traditions appear to conceive of human beings as complex entities that bind together different kinds of essences, breaths, or spirits, which are thought to undergo divergent outcomes after death. It is believed that after death some of these essences may be harmful for living people to encounter without ceremonial protection.

A serious misconception about native North American religions is that, before contact with European civilization, they existed in a changeless "Golden Age" and that what happened later can be described only as degeneration. This view owes much to the misgivings of many 19th-century Europeans over the deep changes wrought on their own societies by the Industrial Age. Change, borrowing, and innovation are characteristic of any living religion, but indigenous communities relied on strands of oral communication to maintain both continuity and the memory of change, and Euro-American observers were ill-equipped to notice and record these sources.

At the same time, the changes that visited Native Americans in the wake of the arrival of the Europeans were massive, unprecedented, and mostly destructive. Whole languages—and with them ceremonies, narratives, and oral libraries of accumulated knowledge about human and natural history and humour—were lost. Even the most earnest and energetic efforts to rejuvenate traditional ways can seem pale and pathetic to those who remember earlier days. Yet some elders reject this pessimism. Instead, they note that there was a community where a snake dance was once performed, but the ceremony became extinct. Anthropologists expressed alarm, but an elder insisted that people should not be disturbed. "If it was lost it was because we didn't need it any more," he said. "If we really need it back again, the snakes will teach it to us again. It was they who taught it to us in the first place."

Sometimes, however, disruption is so catastrophic that individuals and communities must respond with fresh, powerful visions that transplant the germ of past wisdom into entirely new seedbeds. When it succeeds, such inspiration can meld tradition and innovation in surprisingly effective ways. Two such examples are the Native American church, sometimes known as the peyote church, and the Ghost Dance movement.

The Native American church emerged in the mid-19th century when an ancient ritual of central Mexico moved into the United States and blended with Christian influences. It spread, in part, through the medium of government-run Indian schools, and it is the only native religious tradition that has become truly portable, spreading from coast to coast. The Ghost Dance was one of two movements influenced by Christian traditions that announced the imminent return of the dead and the restoration of Native Americans' traditional way of life. Although the Ghost Dance tradition suffered a terrible tragedy at the massacre at Wounded Knee, South Dakota, in 1890, it was for a time a powerful expression of both hope and despair as the Euro-American conquest of the continent neared completion. It also continued in modified form until the 1950s and underwent occasional revivals in the later 20th century.

A third response to religious disintegration involves the creation of American Indian Christian congregations. In some instances conversion to Christianity was enforced, with dire penalties for refusal. In other cases it appears to have been accepted voluntarily, out of sincere devotion to the missionaries and their message. In yet other cases it was probably accepted for a more practical mix of reasons. Often conversion meant an increased chance for physical survival, regardless of how sincere the conversion was.

Once physical survival and a degree of stability had been established, many congregations of Native American Christians recast their faith and practice to include traditional views and values. Kinship obligations, sharing of resources, and a general emphasis on community in preference to individualistic approaches to salvation have been some of these Native Christian adaptations. In some cases traditional language and symbolism have been incorporated into Christian worship as well.

American Indian traditionalists believe that the values, knowledge, narrative traditions, and ritual worlds they were taught, however compromised by historical loss and the demands of modern life, are vital to the survival of their human and other-than-human communities. While it is undeniable that much has already been irrevocably lost, all but the most pessimistic find much to work toward and to fight for in the present. Key issues for the survival of these traditions include access to and control of sacred sites, preservation of Native American languages, return of sacred artifacts, and maintenance of the integrity of religious knowledge and values.

NATIVE AMERICAN SPIRITUALITY

CHAPTER 1

Like all people, the Indians were concerned with day-to-day problems on which their survival depended, such as how to produce enough food, avoid illness, and avoid or win in war. Indian religious beliefs and practices reflected these realities and influenced all aspects of their everyday lives, from educating children to building homes, farming, hunting, warfare, and medicine.

SIMILARITIES AND VARIATIONS

Traditional Indian religions were as diverse as the rest of their cultures, with many unique traits arising in different areas and at different times. Some beliefs, however, were widespread and typical of Indian religion more generally. Most Indians believed in a supernatural force that pervaded all nature. Among the Algonquian peoples, this force was known as *manitou*. The Iroquois called it *orenda*, and the Dakota (Sioux), *wakanda*. This force, commonly called the Creator, was the source of the world and all of the other spirits therein. The other spirits (or souls) inhabited humans as well as animals, plants, rocks, mountains, lakes, the sun, the winds, and other natural objects and phenomena. The Indians thought these spirits helped people that they liked and injured those who offended them. This belief system is called animism. The spirit world also included departed relatives as well as yet-to-be-born human beings. Religion was the way that the Indians related to all these spirits.

ANIMISM

The religious belief that everything on Earth is imbued with a powerful spirit, capable of helping or harming human needs, is called animism. This faith in a universally shared life force was involved in the earliest forms of worship. The concept has survived in many societies, particularly among Native Americans.

The word "animism" is derived from the Latin word *anima*, which means "breath of life," or "soul." Animists believe that all objects share the breath of life. According to their religious practices, all must live in harmony and be treated with equal respect.

In the world of the animist, communication with each spiritual being is vital. Prayers and offerings are given to assure the goodwill of the spirits. Animists also believe that it is sinful to waste any element of a spirit that has sacrificed itself. Native Americans, for example, used every part of the buffalo they killed—for food, fuel, clothing, and shelter.

In some traditions, heaven seems to recede into the background. Native American cultures are oriented toward the totality of earth, sky, and the four directions (north, south, east, west) rather than toward heaven alone. Although heaven is not typically the abode of the blessed dead in Native American mythology, the stars, Sun, Moon, clouds, mountaintops, and sky-dwelling creators figure significantly.

The Christian-influenced prophetic visions characteristic of revitalization movements such as the 19th-century Ghost Dance and the religion of Handsome Lake are fervently millenarian, proclaiming the advent of an eschatological paradise to be accompanied by the return of the dead and the restoration of tribal life.

HANDSOME LAKE

Also called Longhouse Religion, or Gai'wiio (Seneca: "Good Message"), Handsome Lake is the longest-established prophet movement in North America. Its founder was Ganioda'yo, a Seneca chief whose name meant "Handsome Lake." His heavenly revelations received in trance in 1799 rapidly transformed both himself and the demoralized Seneca.

The group's Christian beliefs, which came primarily from Quaker contacts, included a personal creator-ruler, a devil, heaven, hell, and judgment; Jesus was identified with a local mythological figure. Seneca divinities were retained as ruling angels, rituals were reduced to four transformed dance feasts, and the longhouse was modified into a "church." A puritan and modernizing ethic attacked alcohol and witchcraft, banned further land sales, encouraged the men to practice plow agriculture and animal husbandry, and stressed stability of the nuclear family.

Ganioda'yo's teaching spread among the Iroquois and later became embodied in fixed forms as the "Code of Handsome Lake," which is still recited once in two years in the 20th century by authorized "preachers" in some 10 longhouses providing for about 5,000 adherents on Iroquois reservations in New York state in the United States and in Ontario and Quebec in Canada. Though not antiwhite, the religion serves to maintain Indian identity and has shown some growth in the 20th century.

SHAMANS AND PRIESTS

People who had special powers to contact the spirits were known as shamans. They could be men or women of any age from childhood onward. Among many tribes they held a prominent place in society. Shamans acquired their supernatural power through a personal experience, such as a vision or a dream. They usually underwent initiation rituals as well.

Hupa female shaman, photograph by Edward S. Curtis, c. 1923. Edward S. Curtis Collection/Library of Congress, Washington, D.C. (neg. no. LC-USZ62-101261)

Indians believed that shamans could control the weather, foretell the future, bring success in warfare and food gathering, and ease childbirth. But the main task of shamans was healing the sick. For this reason, they were sometimes called medicine men or medicine women. Some treatments included the use of roots and herbs as medicines. But Indians believed that some illnesses could be cured only by removing a foreign object from the body. In these cases the shaman often "removed" a symbolic object, such as a stone or arrowhead, through sleight of hand.

In some tribes shamans were organized into medicine societies. An example was the Iroquois False Face Society, whose members wore masks carved from living trees. In spring and fall they went from house to house shaking turtle-shell rattles and chanting to drive away evil spirits that caused disease. Another example was the Grand Medicine Society, or Midewiwin, of the Ojibwa.

Priests played an important role in the religious life of some tribes. Unlike shamans, who usually worked with individuals, priests performed public ceremonies. Among the Inca, Maya, Aztec, and some Southeast Indians, priests were political as well as spiritual leaders.

CEREMONIES

Villages and tribes used dances and other ceremonies to seek help from spiritual forces. Many of these ceremonies remain a feature of tribal life. Usually men and women conducted different kinds of ceremonies. Because women were usually in charge of farming and gathering plants, their ceremonies were often meant to ensure that harvests would be good. Such women's groups often met as part of the normal workday, in fields or while foraging. They would plan and organize their ceremonies during these times and then perform the rituals in front of the whole community. Men, on the other hand, tended to be involved in ceremonies meant to ensure successful hunting, raiding, and defense. Usually men had a house where secret societies met, sacred objects were kept, and the ceremonies were taught to boys.

Important ceremonies could last for many days and were usually preceded by periods of fasting and prayer. The most spectacular Plains ceremony was the Sun Dance, which was an expression of thanks to the participants' spirit guardians. Corn dances were held by all farming tribes. One of the most elaborate corn festivals was the Green Corn Ceremony, or Busk, held by the Creek and other Southeast peoples.

Painting by artist John White, depicting a harvest-related dance—possibly the Green Corn dance—conducted by American Indians of the Carolina coast. © The Trustees of the British Museum/Art Resource, NY

After feasting on the new corn, dancing, drinking the "black drink" (which made one vomit), and carrying on ceremonies for several days, the tribe began a new year by destroying old equipment and getting new. They extinguished fires and lit new ones from a ceremonial flame. Old enmities were forgotten and wrongdoers forgiven.

State-level societies generally made sacrifices, or offerings, to gain favor of the gods. The sacrifice could be an object, a plant, an animal, or a human. The Aztec sacrificed thousands of people each year by offering their hearts to the sun god. Some Inca rituals also included human sacrifice.

VISION QUEST

Many Indians believed that every individual could have a personal relationship with one or more spirits. When faced with a critical problem or decision, they generally sought help from the spirit world. The most common way to seek help was to undertake a vision quest. Many people tried their first vision quest as they entered adolescence, at about age 10 to 15.

The quest typically involved fasting and praying for several days in an isolated location. In some cultures the participant would watch for an animal that behaved in a significant or unusual way. In others the participant discovered an object (often a stone) that resembled some animal. In the most common form, the person had a dream (the vision) in which a spirit-being appeared. Upon receiving a sign or vision, the person returned home and sought help in interpreting the experience.

Among many peoples, the spirit that appeared in the vision quest became the participant's lifelong totem, guardian, or adviser. Such spirit-beings were usually animals. The Northwest Coast wood-carvers put the sacred animals onto totem poles, while Plains Indians painted them on tepees.

AMERICAN INDIAN FOLKLORE

The folklore that was here when the Europeans came was, of course, that of the American Indian. It was made up of tales about animals, witches, little people, good spirits, and ugly spirits. In a number of ways it was connected with the religion of the Indians, and there is no sharp dividing line between their religious myths and their folktales. Indian folklore also included many songs and dances that were part of Indian festivals. Such songs and dances usually had a religious meaning.

The Indian had a real feeling of thanks to the Great Spirit for his blessings, and this feeling was a part of daily life. If the Indian killed a buffalo for meat, he thanked the spirit of the buffalo for the use of the meat. He was grateful to the maple trees for the sweet water they poured out to him in the spring of the year and from which he could make maple syrup. He thanked the green corn for its sweet ears. He thanked the spirits who had planted the juicy red strawberries for his enjoyment. He sang and danced his thankfulness and often told stories of how the good things and the bad things of life came to be.

Many American Indians tell these stories even now. They tell of the old woman who lives on top of a high mountain. After the old moon has reached its fullness, she cuts it up into little stars and she strews them all across the heavens. Sometimes the Indians of the Six Nations, the Iroquois, hold their religious rites at night in the Long House. In the darkness they beat upon drums and dance for the little people, who join them only when they cannot be seen.

NATURE
WORSHIP

I n the history of religions and cultures, nature worship, which is a system of religion based on the veneration of natural phenomena, has not been well documented. Among the indigenous peoples of many countries, including Native Americans, the concept of nature as a totality is unknown; only individual natural phenomena—e.g., stars, rain, and animals—are comprehended as natural objects or forces that influence them and are thus in some way worthy of being venerated or placated. Nature as an entity in itself, in contrast with human society and culture or even with God, is a philosophical or poetic conception that has been developed among advanced civilizations. This concept of nature worship, therefore, is limited primarily to scholars involved in or influenced by the modern (especially Western) study of religion.

NATURE AS A SACRED TOTALITY

To students of religion, the closest example of what may be termed *nature worship* is perhaps most apparent in ancient cultures in which there is a high god as the lord in heaven who has withdrawn from the immediate details of the governing of the world. This kind of high god—the *deus otiosus*, Latin for "hidden, or idle, god"—is one who has delegated all work on earth to what are called "nature spirits," which are the forces or personifications of the forces of nature. High gods exist, for example, in such indigenous religions on Africa's west coast as that of the Dyola of Guinea. In such religions the human spiritual environment is functionally structured by means of per-sonified natural powers, or nature spirits.

The power or force within nature that has most often been venerated, worshiped, or held in holy awe is mana. Often designated as "impersonal power" or "supernatural power," the term mana used by Polynesians and Melanesians was appropriated by 19th-century Western anthropologists and applied to that which affected the common processes of nature. Mana was conceptually linked to North American Indian terms that conveyed the same or similar notions—e.g., *orenda* of the Iroquois, *wakan* of the Dakotas, and *manitou* of the Algonquin. Neither "impersonal power" nor "supernatural power" implies the true meaning of mana, however, because mana usually issues from persons or is used by them, and the concept of a supernatural sphere as distinct or separate from a natural sphere is seldom recognized by the peoples who use the term.

Thus, a better designation for mana is "super force" or "extraordinary efficiency." A person who has mana is successful, fortunate, and demonstrates extraordinary skill—e.g., as an artisan, warrior, or chief. Mana can also be obtained from the *atuas* (gods), provided that they themselves possess it.

The Iroquoian term *orenda*, like mana, designates a power that is inherent in numerous objects of nature but that does not have essential personification or animistic elements. Orenda, however, is not a collective omnipotence. Powerful hunters, priests, and shamans have *orenda* to some degree. The *wakanda*, or *wakan*, of the Sioux is described similarly, but as Wakan-Tanka it may refer to a collective unity of gods with great power (*wakan*). The *manitou* of the Algonquin is not, like *wakan*, merely an impersonal power that is inherent in all things of nature but is also the personification of numerous manitous

Sioux warrior Turning Bear. Some chiefs and warriors were thought to possess "mana," a powerful force bestowed by nature upon certain individuals. The Sioux variation was known by the term "wakan." Library of Congress Prints and Photographs Division

(powers), with a Great Manitou (Kitchi-Manitou) at the head. These *manitous* may even be designated as protective spirits akin to those of other North American Indians, such as the *digi* of the Apache, *boha* of the Shoshone, and *maxpe* of the Crow, as well as the *sila* of the Eskimo.

HEAVEN AND EARTH AS SACRED SPACES, FORCES, OR PROCESSES

Heaven and earth, as personified powers of nature and thus worthy of worship, are evidently not of equal age. Although from earliest times heaven was believed to be the residence of a high being or a prominent god, the earth as a personified entity is much rarer; it probably first occurred among archaic agrarian civilizations, and it continues to occur in some less industrialized societies in which agriculture is practiced. Gods of heaven, however, are characteristic spiritual beings of early and contemporary hunting and gathering societies and are found in almost all cultures.

Some worldviews generally assume the earth to be simply given (i.e., as continuously existing). Sometimes the earth is believed to have emerged out of chaos or a primal sea or to have come into existence by the act of a heavenly god, transformer, or demiurge (creator). Even in these worldviews, however, the earth usually remains without a divine owner, unless through agriculture and the cult of the dead the earth is conceived as the source of the renewing powers of nature or as the underworld.

HEAVEN

The fact that heaven is animated by rain-giving clouds (with lightning and thunder) and by a regular chorus of warming and illuminating celestial bodies (sun, moon,

In Native American culture, lightning strikes are believed to originate from the beak of the thunderbird, a mythological creature that waters vegetation so it can grow. Jeremy Woodhouse/Photodisc/Getty Images

and stars) led to concepts of the personification of heaven from earliest times. Heavenly deities, as the personification of the physical aspects of the sky, appear in variations that are adapted to the types of cultures concerned.

THE FATHER OF THE FAMILY

The god of heaven is often viewed as an ever active father of the family, often called upon but rarely the recipient of sacrifices. He is able to intervene in human and natural affairs without the aid of an intermediary—e.g., priest, medicine man, or ancestors. As a numinous (spiritual) being, he is closer to humanity than other spiritual powers are. He sends lightning and rain and rules the stars

29

that are at most essential aspects of himself or are members of his family subject to him. He is the creator and the receiver of the dead. Very human, often comical, or even unethical and repulsive traits of such deities are often represented in myths that also sometimes include legends of animal or human ancestors.

This type of deity is generally found in its most developed form among the old hunting and gathering peoples of the temperate and arid areas, including North American forest dwellers. Among such peoples, heaven is often merged with an old hunting deity, the lord of the animals, or it allows the latter to exist as a hypostasis by his side.

THE GOD OF HEAVEN VIEWED DUALISTICALLY

In several religions the god of heaven has an antagonistic evil adversary who delights in destroying completely or partially the good creative deeds of the god of heaven. This helps to explain the insecurity of existence and concepts of ethical dualism. In most such cases, the contrasts experienced in the relationship between heaven and earth deities have been reevaluated along ethical lines by means of exalting the heavenly elements at the expense of the earthly ones (especially in Jewish, Christian, and Islamic sects in Europe, west-central and northern Asia, and certain areas of northern Africa). The figure of an antagonistic trickster or demiurge that has a somewhat ethical component may be the result of diffusion and is rather rare in such cultures as those of the Khoisan and the indigenous peoples of Australia and North America.

EARTH

Although in polytheistic religions the earth is usually represented as a goddess and associated with the god of heaven as her spouse, only rarely is there an elaborate or intensive cult of earth worship. There are in many religions mother goddesses who have elaborate cults and who have assumed the function of fertility for land and human beings, but they hardly have a chthonic (earth) basis. Some mother goddesses, such as Inanna-Ishtar, instead have a heavenly, astral origin. There are, however, subordinate figures of various pantheons, such as Nerthus in Germanic religion or Demeter and Persephone (earth mother and corn girl) in Greek religion, who have played greater roles than Gaea (the world mother). Among Indo-Europeans, western Asians (despite their various fertility deities), Chinese, Koreans, and Japanese, the gods of heaven, sun, and thunderstorms have held a paramount interest.

When the common people have displayed intensive attention to "mother earth" (such as the practice of laying down newborn babies on the earth and many other rites), this partially reflects older cults that have remained relatively free from warrior and nation-building peoples with their emphasis on war (as in western Sudan, pre-Vedic India, and the Indian agrarian area of northern Mexico). The Andean earth-mother figure, Pachamama (Pacha Mama), worshiped by the Peruvians, stands in sharp contrast to the sun religion of the Inca (the conquering lord of the Andes region). Earth deities are most actively venerated in areas in which people are closely bound to ancestors and to the cultivation of grain.

Mountains

Especially prominent mountains are favourite places for cults of high places, particularly when they are isolated as island mountains, mountains with snowcaps, or uninhabited high mountain ranges. The psychological roots of the cults of high places lie in the belief that mountains are close to the sky (as heavenly ladders), that clouds surrounding the mountaintops are givers of rain, and that mountains with volcanoes form approaches to the fiery insides of the earth.

Mountains, therefore, serve as the abodes of the gods, as the centres of the dead who live underground, as burial places for rainmakers (medicine men), and as places of oracles for soothsayers. In cosmogenic (origin of the world) myths, mountains are the first land to emerge from the primeval water. They frequently become the cosmic mountain (i.e., the world conceived as a mountain) that is symbolically represented by a small hill on which a king stands at the inauguration. Pilgrimages to mountain altars or shrines are favourite practices of cults of high places. The larger mountain ranges and canyons between volcanic mountains—including the mountainous areas of North and South America (the Rocky Mountains, the Andes)— are most often centres of cults of high places.

EARTHQUAKES

According to the beliefs of many peoples, earthquakes originate in mountains. In some areas a bearer who holds the world up—a concept that probably came from Arabia, Persia, or India—is believed to cause an earthquake when he changes his position or when he moves his burden from one shoulder to the other. World bearers often are giants or heroes, such as Atlas, but they also may be animals, such as a turtle (America).

TIDES

The view that the tides are caused by the moon can be found over almost all the earth. This regular natural phenomenon seldom gives rise to cults, but the ebb and flow of the coastal waters have stimulated mythological concepts. Not infrequently the moon acquires the status of a water deity because of this phenomenon. The Tlingit of the northwestern United States view the moon as an old woman, the mistress of the tides. The animal hero and trickster Yetl, the raven, is successful in conquering (with the aid of the mink) the seashore from the moon at low tide, and thus an extended area is gained for nourishment with small sea animals.

CELESTIAL PHENOMENA AS OBJECTS OF WORSHIP OR VENERATION

A form of mythology based on the most visible of the heavenly bodies is common in certain polytheistic belief systems, including many Native American cultures. Prominent among these objects of heavenly worship are the sun and the moon. Myths of human descent from a sun god are known among some North American Indian tribes, including the Arapaho and Blackfeet. The moon—because it appears, disappears, and appears again—was believed by some peoples to be the first human who died. In some cases the moon god was viewed as one who had taken the place of a Supreme Being.

THE SUN

Generally, the sun is worshiped more in colder regions and the moon in warm regions. Also, the sun is usually considered as male and the moon as female. Exceptions to these generalizations, however, are notable, including the conception of the female sun ruling parts of North America. The Natchez Indians of the southeastern United States, who are culturally connected with Central America, called their king "Great Sun" and the noblemen "the Suns."

The sun in some religions is conceived as a purely mythical being, cultically recognized in sun dances such as those of prairie-dwelling Native Americans and in

The New Mexico state flag, featuring a sun symbol of the Zia, a Pueblo tribe that resides in the state, at its centre. fstockfoto/Shutterstock.com

various celebrations of the solstice. These rites may be either survivals of an earlier local cult of a sun deity or influences of such a cult.

THE MOON

The moon is often personified in different ways and worshiped with ritual customs; nevertheless, in contrast to the sun, the moon is less frequently viewed as a powerful deity. It appears to be of great importance as the basis of a lunar calendar but not in more advanced agrarian civilizations. The moon, infrequently associated with the highest god, is usually placed below heaven and the sun.

person by being addressed with kinship terms that had been used for the deceased.

Traditionally, all people were in contact with the spirit world. They carried objects called amulets, which were believed to have special powers to protect or bring good fortune. All people also experienced dreams and achieved special relationships with particular spirit-beings. Men and women who had an especially strong connection with the spirits became shamans. They were called on to cure the sick by recovering lost souls, to foretell the future, to determine the location of game, and so forth.

Arctic peoples took great care not to offend the spirits of game animals, since they could bring on sickness or famine. Therefore, there arose complicated systems of regulations concerning the preparation of food, all with the purpose of keeping harmony between people and the environment. In addition, courtesies given to freshly killed animals promoted their reincarnation as new animals of the same species.

Subarctic

Subarctic peoples traditionally had a highly individualistic relationship with the supernatural: most men and women undertook a vision quest in their youth and relied heavily upon one or more guardian spirits for protection and guidance. In Kaska terms the vision occurred by "dreaming of animals in a lonely place" or hearing "somebody sing," perhaps a moose in the guise of a person. Dreams notified an individual of impending events and might advise one how to behave in order to achieve success or avoid misfortune.

Among many Subarctic peoples there was a widespread belief that hunting success depended upon treating

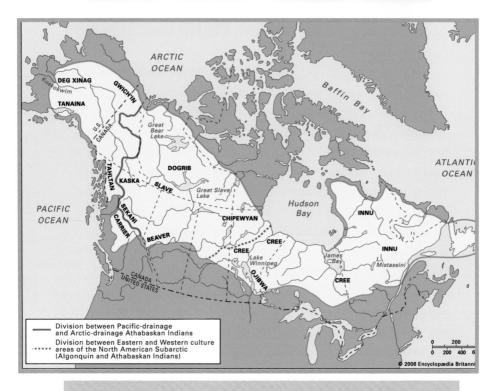

Distribution of American Subarctic cultures. Encyclopedia Britannica, Inc.

prey animals and their remains with reverence. This involved various practices such as disposing of the animals' bones carefully so that dogs could not chew them. Respect was particularly evident in the use of polite circumlocutions to refer to bears. Many groups undertook several ceremonial observances in bear hunting, including a purifying sweat bath before departing on the hunt and an offer of tobacco to a bear that had been killed. Afterward the people feasted and danced in its honour.

Two important concepts of the Innu and other Algonquian groups were *manitou* and the "big man" (a concept quite different from the "big men" of Melanesian cultures, who are local leaders). *Manitou* represents a pervasive power in the world that individuals can learn to use on their own behalf. The term "Great Manitou," designating a personal god, probably represents a missionary-inspired adaptation of an older idea. A person's big man is an intimate spirit-being who confers wisdom, competence, skill, and strength in the food quest as well as in other areas of life, including magic. Maintaining a relationship with this being requires ethically good conduct. Animal-spirit "bosses" who control the supply of caribou, fish, and other creatures are another traditional belief shared by Algonquian and certain Athabaskan groups.

Three of the most popular characters in Algonquian folklore are Wiitiko (Windigo), a terrifying cannibalistic giant apt to be encountered in the forest; Tcikapis, a kindly, powerful young hero and the subject of many myths; and Wiskijan (Whiskeyjack), an amusing trickster. "Wiitiko psychosis" refers to a condition in which an individual would be seized by the obsessive idea that he was turning into a cannibal with a compulsive craving for human flesh.

TRICKSTER TALES

Trickster tales are stories featuring a protagonist (often an anthropomorphized animal) who has magical powers and is characterized as a compendium of opposites. Simultaneously an omniscient creator and an innocent fool, a malicious destroyer and a childlike prankster, the trickster-hero serves as a sort of folkloric scapegoat onto which are projected the fears, failures, and unattained ideals of the source culture. North American trickster motifs generally combine moral lessons with humour.

Trickster stories may be told for amusement as well as on serious or sacred occasions. Depending on the context, either a single tale or a series of interrelated stories might be told. The typical tale recounts a picaresque adventure: the trickster is "going along," encounters a situation to which he responds with knavery, stupidity, gluttony, or guile (or, most often, some combination of these), and meets a violent or ludicrous end. Often the trickster serves as a transformer and culture hero who creates order out of chaos. He may teach humans the skills of survival, such as how to make fire, procreate, or catch or raise food, usually through negative examples that end with his utter failure to accomplish these tasks. Frequently he is accompanied by a companion who either serves as a stooge or ultimately tricks the trickster.

Shamanism was an important feature of traditional Subarctic culture. The shaman, who could be male or female, served as a specialist curer and diviner in addition to his or her routine adult responsibilities. It was thought that occasionally shamans became evil and behaved malignantly. Shamanistic ability came to an individual from dreaming of animals who taught the dreamer to work with their aid; such ability had to be validated through successful performance.

The Deg Xinag conceived of humans as comprising body, soul, and "speech," the latter an element surviving after death but, unlike the soul, not reincarnated. Hazards to life came from the soul always being menaced by various supernatural figures that were the primary enemies of human survival and by the souls of powerful evil shamans acting on behalf of these supernatural figures. In contrast, spirit-beings associated with animals and berries supported human survival. Animal songs and amulets created good relations with helpful animal spirits; elaborate ceremonies in the men's house, to which the spirit-beings were invited, protected the food supply.

SOUL LOSS

Certain Native American tribes believe in the concept of soul loss, wherein the soul departs from the body and fails to return. In many preliterate cultures soul loss is believed to be a primary cause of illness and death.

In some cultures individuals are believed to have one soul that may wander inadvertently when its owner's guard is relaxed, as when asleep, sneezing, or yawning. Other cultures believe that each person has two or more souls, usually including a "wandering" soul that experiences one's dreams and a "life" soul that maintains one's corporeal vitality. The most dangerous instances of soul loss involve malevolent witchcraft and the enticement and capture of a soul in order to cause harm to its owner.

Those who believe in soul loss hold that an owner can prevent the soul from wandering by means of ritual utterances, such as saying "God bless" when one sneezes, or by a variety of supernatural means, such as the wearing of charms or ingesting of magical substances. However, in cases where the soul's owner believes he or she has been bewitched, soul retrieval requires complex techniques and the services of a religious specialist. The essence of most cures is the catching of the lost soul by a shaman and its reintroduction into the patient's body.

Northeast Indians

Animism—the belief that everything has a soul or spirit—pervaded many aspects of life for the Northeast tribes. It was expressed in a wide variety of ways. Among many upper Great Lakes tribes, each clan owned a bundle of sacred objects. Together the objects in the bundle were seen as spirit-beings that were in some sense alive. The clan was responsible for performing the rituals that insured those beings' health and goodwill. The Iroquois had no comparable clan ceremonies. Instead, a significant part of their ritual life centered on ceremonies in recognition of foods as they matured. These rituals included festivals celebrating the maple, strawberry, bean, and green corn harvests, as well as a midwinter ceremony.

Medicine societies were also important. They were so named because one of their major functions was curing and because their membership consisted of people who had undergone such cures. Typically their practices combined the use of medicinal plants with what would now be considered psychiatric care or psychological support. The most famous medicine society among the upper Great Lakes Algonquians was the Midewiwin, or Grand Medicine Society. Its elaborate annual or semiannual meetings included the performance of various magical feats. Of the various Iroquois medicine societies, the False Face Society is perhaps best known. The wooden masks worn by members of this society during their rituals were carved from living trees. The masks were believed to be powerful living beings capable of curing the sick when properly cared for or of causing great harm when treated disrespectfully.

Not all curing was performed by members of medicine societies. Shamans had the power to cure, a power that was often indicated in a vision or dream. Dreams were especially important. They indicated not only the causes of illness and an individual's power to cure but also the means of maintaining good fortune in various aspects of life. They might indicate whether one had special ability in warfare, hunting, and other such activities. So much attention was paid to dreams that among some peoples a mother asked her children each morning if they had dreamed in order to teach them to pay attention to these experiences. Dreams could also influence the decisions of councils.

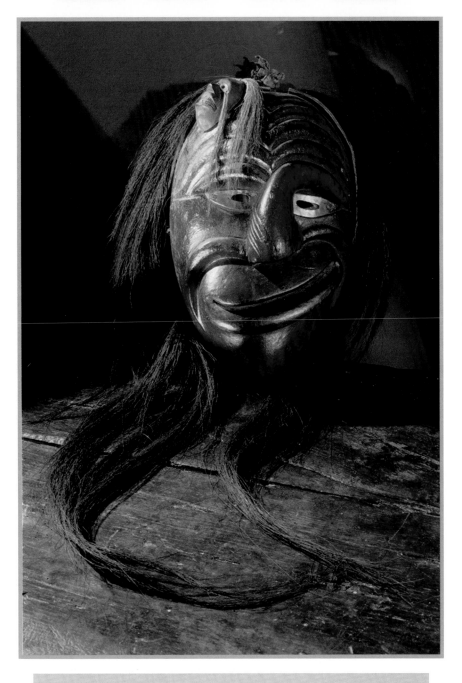

Ceremonial mask used by members of the False Face Society. Werner Forman/
Art Resource, NY

Boys in Northeast tribes sometimes undertook a vision quest, though this ritual was not as important in the Northeast as it was among the Plains Indians. The goal of a vision quest was to receive a sign from a supernatural being. A shaman then helped to interpret the vision. Girls typically went through a period of isolation and training when they experienced their first menstruation.

SOUTHEAST INDIANS

The delicate relationship between humans and the natural world is well expressed in what is known of traditional Southeast religions and worldviews. These emphasized animism, a perspective in which humans share the world with a proliferation of spiritual essences of animals, plants, and natural objects or phenomena.

The peoples of this region believed that animals possessed souls. Slain animals sought vengeance against humanity through the agency of their "species chief," a supernatural animal with great power. The Deer Chief, for instance, was able to exact revenge on humans who dishonoured his people—the deer—during the hunt. Hunting thus became a sacred act and was much imbued with taboo, ritual, and sacrifice. Most disease was attributed to failures in placating the souls of slain animals.

The plant world was considered friendly to humans, and the Cherokees thought that every animal-sent disease could be cured by a corresponding plant antidote. The economic significance of corn was memorialized by the near universality of the Green Corn Ceremony, or Busk, throughout the Southeast. This was a major ceremonial suffused with an ethos of annual renewal in which the sacred fire—and often the hearth fires of each home—was rekindled; old debts and grudges were forgiven and forgotten; old clothing and stored food were discarded; and a sense of community was regenerated.

Spiritual power could reside in objects other than plants and animals. Medicine men possessed sacred stones, quartz crystals, and other mystically endowed paraphernalia. Other objects were consecrated to symbolize the collective solidarity of the group. The Cherokees made use of a palanquin or litter within which were placed revered objects; the Tukabahchee Creeks possessed sacred embossed copper plates; and the temples of several Lower Mississippi tribes contained an assortment of idols and icons. Natural objects could be infused with sacred power in a variety of ways, including contact with thunder, as in lightning-struck wood; immersion in a rapidly flowing stream; and exposure to the smoke of the sacred fire or of ritually prepared tobacco.

The outlines of a formal theology can be discerned from early accounts of some of the stratified societies and from those tribes that survived the immediate ravages of European contact. Most groups possessed origin myths, often involving a primal deluge into which prototypical beings plunged to secure a portion of mud that magically expanded to create the Earth, which was often viewed as an island. The subsequent course of mythological history was frequently related in terms of a cosmic struggle between a celestial culture hero who bestowed boons on humankind and an underworld antihero who became the source of the fatality and misfortune inherent in the human condition. Southeastern myths and folktales are populated by a myriad of nature spirits, monsters, tricksters, giants, and little people.

Among many tribes, evidence survives that suggests belief in a supreme being, sometimes depicted as the master of breath. This ultimate divinity was frequently associated with the sun and its earthly aspect, fire. In addition, the world was viewed as quadrisected by the cardinal directions; each direction had a presiding spirit and appropriate colour symbolism. Concern with the remote supreme being seems to have rested more with the priesthood than with the everyday activities of the average individual. The life of the latter was more intimately tied up with the proximal spiritual beings who were felt to intervene more directly in human affairs.

In some of the wealthier stratified societies, priests were given specialized training and became full-time religious practitioners responsible for the spiritual health of the community. Priests also assumed the responsibility of conducting the major collective religious rituals that punctuated the calendrical cycle. Complementary to the priesthood were various individual magico-medical practitioners, such as sorcerers, conjurors, diviners, herbalists, and healers, who were generally part-time specialists and catered to individual needs and crises, especially the treatment of illness. Medical therapy was intricately enmeshed in the spiritual view of the world and might include such practical procedures as isolation, sweating, bathing, bloodletting, sucking, the inducement of vomiting, the internal and external application of herbal medicines, and the recitation of ritual chants.

The frequent elaboration of funerary practices, including interring the chiefly dead with great quantities of freshwater pearls and other rare materials, indicates that most groups believed in an afterlife. It was generally thought that the souls of the recently deceased would hover around the community and try to induce close friends and relatives to join them in their journey to eternity; thus, the elaborate funerary rites and the extensive taboos associated with death were as much a protection for the living as a commemoration of the dead. This was especially the case because death was never considered a natural event but was always the result of malevolent animal spirits, witches, or the deadly machinations of sorcerers. If a death had been caused by human agents, the soul of the deceased would never rest until vengeance had been secured by its living relatives. Once appeased, the soul moved to a final resting place, the location of which varied from group to group; typically, this was either in the direction of the setting sun, in the celestial firmament, or in a non-hellish part of the underworld.

PLAINS INDIANS

Plains peoples generally believed in animism—the idea that animals, plants, the sun, moon, stars, and all other natural phenomena are inhabited by spirit-beings. Success in life was thought to depend on the intervention of these spirit-beings. The usual procedure for obtaining spirit help was to undertake a vision quest, in which a person would go to an isolated spot to fast and beg for aid. If the quest was successful, the spirit-being would give instructions for winning in battle, curing illness, or obtaining other skills or powers. The quest for supernatural power through a vision or dream was important among all of the tribes and among both girls and boys. Vision quests were often begun when a child was as young as six or seven years old.

All Plains tribes had people who communicated with the spirit world to perform acts of healing. In most groups ordinary illnesses such as headaches would be treated with common herbal remedies, while a shaman would be called in to treat more serious illnesses. Shamans could also locate enemies and game animals and find lost objects. Arapaho, Atsina, and Cheyenne shamans were said to walk on fire as a proof of their powers.

Some Plains peoples, including the Cheyenne, the Atsina, and the Pawnee, believed in a supreme spirit. The Cheyenne, for example, held that "the Wise One above" knew better than all other creatures; further, he had long ago left Earth and retired to the sky. In smoking ceremonies the first offering of the pipe was always made to him. Some other tribes, such as the Crow, believed instead in many gods, each of whom possessed about equal power.

Ceremonies and rituals were widespread on the Plains. They ranged from very simple rites to complicated events involving weeks of preparation and performances that lasted for several days. A number of common ritual elements were used alone or combined in various ways. Packages called medicine bundles figured prominently in rituals throughout the region. They held objects that were believed to have supernatural power, such as the sacred pipe. Some medicine bundles belonged to individuals; others belonged to the entire tribe and were kept by chiefs or shamans.

The most important religious ceremony on the Plains was the Sun Dance. It was practiced by both villagers and nomads. It was held once a year in summer, when the whole tribe could gather. Although the whole community took part, only one or a few individuals were pledged to undertake the ritual. Weeks or even months were needed for spiritual preparation and to gather the food, gifts, and other materials the pledges and their families were expected to provide. As the community gathered, a dance structure was built in the center of the camp circle or village. It had a central pole that symbolized a connection to the divine, as embodied by the sun. The pledges and other participants fasted and danced for several days, praying for power. In some tribes a ritual leader pinched some skin on the pledge's breast or back, pierced through it with a sharp instrument, and inserted a wooden skewer through the piercing. One end of a rope was tied to the skewer, and the other end was attached to the center pole. The dancer leaned back until the line was taut and strained until the line tore through his piercings. This act of self-sacrifice was supposed to bring good fortune to the tribe.

SOUTHWEST INDIANS

Like most Indian religions, those of the Southwest Indians were generally characterized by animism and shamanism. Animists believe that spirit-beings animate the sun, moon, rain, thunder, animals, plants, and many other

Members of the Kainah, or Blood, tribe performing a dance during Sun Dance ceremonies in Alberta, Canada. National Film Board of Canada/ Archive Photos/Getty Images

natural phenomena. Shamans were men and women who achieved supernatural knowledge or power to treat physical and spiritual ailments. Shamans had to be very aware of the community's goings-on or risk the consequences. For example, a number of accounts from the 1800s report the execution of Pima shamans who were believed to have caused people to sicken and die.

The spectacular Pueblo ceremonies for rain and growth reflected a conception of the universe in which every person, animal, plant, and supernatural being was considered significant. Without the active participation of every individual in the group, it was believed that the life-giving sun would not return from his "winter house" after the solstice, the rain would not fall, and the crops would not grow. In fact, Pueblo groups generally believed that the cosmic order was always in danger of breaking down and that an annual cycle of ceremonies was crucial to the continued existence of the world.

According to the Pueblo, humans affected the world through their actions, emotions, and attitudes. Communities that encouraged harmony were visited by spirit-beings called kachinas each year. In ceremonies men in elaborate regalia impersonated the kachinas to call forth the spirits. The kachina religion was most common among the western Pueblos and was less important to the east.

The Apache believed that the universe was inhabited by a great variety of powerful beings, including animals, plants, witches (evil shamans), superhuman beings, rocks, and mountains. All could affect the world for good or ill. The Apache talked to, sung to, scolded, or praised each one. Ceremonies appealed to these powerful beings for aid in curing disease and for success in hunting and warfare.

Dolls representing various kachinas, or ancestral spirits that interact with humans. The dolls are used to teach the identities of the kachinas to young girls of Pueblo tribes. The Bridgeman Art Library/Getty Images

Navajo ceremonies were based on a similar view of the universe. The Navajo believed that power resided in a great many beings that were dangerous and unpredictable. These belonged to two classes: Earth Surface People (human beings, ghosts, and witches) and Holy People (supernaturals who could aid Earth Surface People or harm them by sending sickness). As they turned away from hunting and raiding in favor of farming and herding, the Navajo focused their attention on elaborate rituals or "sings." These aimed to cure sickness and bring an individual into harmony with his family group, nature, and the spirit world.

In contrast to the animistic religions of other Southwest tribes, the River Yumans believed in a supreme being that was the source of all supernatural power. Dreams were the only way to acquire the supernatural protection, guidance, and power that were considered necessary for success in life. Traditional myths seen in dreams were turned into songs and acted out in ceremonies. The spiritual quest sometimes caused an individual religious or war leader to abandon all other activities—farming, food collecting, and even hunting.

The religion of the Tohono O'odham shared features with those of both the River Yumans and the Pueblo. Like the River Yumans, they "sang for power" and went on individual vision quests. Like the Pueblo, they also held communal ceremonies to keep the world in order.

GREAT BASIN PEOPLES

Religious concepts derived from a mythical cosmogony, beliefs in powerful spirit-beings, and a belief in a dualistic soul. Mythology provided a cosmogony and cosmography of the world in which anthropomorphic animal progenitors, notably Wolf, Coyote, Rabbit, Bear, and Mountain Lion, were supposed to have lived before the human age. During that period they were able to speak and act as humans do; they created the world and were responsible for present-day topography, ecology, food resources, seasons of the year, and distribution of tribes. They set the nature of social relations—that is, they defined how various classes of kin should behave toward each other—and set the customs surrounding birth, marriage, puberty, and death. Their actions in the mythic realm set moral and ethical precepts and determined the physical and behavioral characteristics of the modern animals. Most of the motifs and tale plots of Great Basin mythology are found widely throughout North America.

Spirit-beings were animals, birds, or natural or supernatural phenomena, each thought to have a specific power according to an observed characteristic. Some such beings were thought to be benevolent, or at least neutral, toward humans. Others, such as water babies—small long-haired creatures who lured people to their death in springs or lakes and who ate children—were malevolent and feared. Great Basin peoples also had conceptions of a variety of other beings, such as the Southern Paiute *unupits*, mischievous spirits who caused illness.

Shamanism was prominent in all Great Basin groups. Both men and women might become shamans. One was called to shamanism by a spirit-being who came unsought; it was considered dangerous to resist this call, for those who did sometimes died. The being became a tutelary guide, instructing an individual in curing and sources of power. Some shamans had several tutelary spirit-beings, each providing instruction for specific practices, such as the power to cure disease, to foretell the future, or to practice sorcery. Among Northern Paiute and Washoe and probably elsewhere, a person who had received power became an apprentice to an older, practicing shaman and from that mentor learned a variety of rituals, cures, and feats of legerdemain associated with curing performances. Curing ceremonies were performed with family members and others present and might last several days. The widespread Native American practice of sucking an object said to cause the disease from the patient's body was often employed. Shamans who lost too many patients were sometimes killed.

In the western Great Basin, some men were thought to have powers to charm antelope and so led communal antelope drives. Beliefs that some men were arrow-proof (and, after the introduction of guns, bulletproof) are reported for the Northern Paiute and Gosiute but were probably general throughout the area. Among the Eastern Shoshone, young men sought contact with spirit-beings by undertaking the vision quest. The Eastern Shoshone probably learned this practice from their Plains neighbours, although the characteristics of the beings sought were those common to Great Basin beliefs.

There was a concept of soul dualism among most, if not all, Numic peoples. One soul, or soul aspect, represented vitality or life; the other represented the individual as he was in a dream or vision state. During dreams or visions, the latter soul left the body and moved in the spirit realm; at those times, the person could be subject to soul loss. At death, both souls left the body. Death rites were usually minimal; an individual was buried with his possessions, or they were destroyed. The Washoe traditionally abandoned or burned a dwelling in which a death had occurred.

California Indian

Native California's traditional religious institutions were intensely and intimately associated with its political, economic, social, and legal systems. Frequently the priests, shamans, and ritualists in a community organized themselves around one of two religious systems: the Kuksu in the north and the Toloache in the south. Both involved the formal indoctrination of initiates and—potentially, depending upon the individual—a series of subsequent status promotions within the religious society; these processes could literally occupy initiates, members, and mentors throughout their lifetimes. Members of these religious societies exercised considerable economic, political, and social influence in the community.

In the Kuksu religion (common among the Pomo, Yuki, Maidu, and Wintun), colourful and dramatic costumes and equipment were used during ritual impersonations of specific spirit-beings. Within the Toloache religion (as among the Luiseño and Diegueño), initiates performed while drinking a hallucinogenic decoction made of the jimsonweed plant (*Datura meteloides*); the drug put them in a trance and provided them with supernatural knowledge about their future lives and roles as members of the sacred societies.

Closeup image of a jimsonweed plant. A hallucinogenic drink made from the plant's leaves is consumed by certain California tribes during religious rituals. Sam Abell/National Geographic Image Collection/Getty Images

Religions on the Colorado River differed slightly because they were not concerned with developing formal organizations and recruitment procedures. Individuals received religious information through dreams, and members recited long narrative texts, explaining the creation of the world, the travel of culture heroes, and the adventures of historic figures.

In the northwestern part of the culture area, there was another type of informally structured religious system. Its rituals concerned world renewal (as in the white-deerskin dance) and involved the recitation of myths that were privately owned—that is, for which the prerogative of recitation belonged to only a few individuals. One communal need served by these ceremonies was the reification (or, sometimes, restructuring) of relationships. The display of costumes and valuable possessions (such as white deerskins or delicately chipped obsidian blades) reaffirmed social ranking, and the success of the ritual reaffirmed the orderly relationship of humanity to the supernatural.

The use of supernatural power to control events or transform reality was basic to every California group. Generally magic was used in attempts to control the weather, increase the harvest of crops, and foretell the future. Magic or sorcery was deemed not only the cause of sickness and death but also the principal means of curing many diseases. Its practices were also considered to be ways to protect oneself, to punish wrongdoers, and to satisfy personal ends

NORTHWEST

The religions of the Northwest Coast shared several concepts that provided the widespread bases for various kinds of religious activity. One concept was that salmon were supernatural beings who voluntarily assumed piscine form each year in order to sacrifice themselves for the benefit of humankind. On being caught, these spirit-beings returned to their home beneath the sea, where they were reincarnated if their bones or offal were returned to the water. If offended, however, they would refuse to return to the river. Hence, there were numerous specific prohibitions on acts believed to offend them and a number of observances designed to propitiate them, chief of which was the first-salmon ceremony.

This rite varied in detail but invariably involved honouring the first salmon of the main fishing season by sprinkling them with eagle down, red ochre, or some other sacred substance, welcoming them in a formal speech, cooking them, and distributing their flesh, or morsels of it, communion-fashion, to all the members of the local group and any guests. The maximal elaboration of this rite occurred in northwestern California in what have been called world-renewal ceremonies; these combined first-salmon rituals, first-fruits observances, and dances in which lineage wealth was displayed. Elsewhere the first-salmon rituals were less elaborate but still important, except among the Tlingit, who did not perform them.

Another religious concept was the acquisition of personal power by seeking individual contact with a spirit-being, usually through prayer and a vision. Among Coast Salish all success in life—whether in hunting, woodworking, accumulating wealth, military ventures, or magic—was bestowed by spirit-beings encountered in the vision quest. From these entities each person acquired songs, special regalia, and dances. Collectively, the dances constituted the major ceremonials of the Northwest

Coast peoples; known as the spirit dances, they were performed during the winter months.

In the Wakashan and northern provinces, it was believed that remote ancestors who had undertaken vision quests had been rewarded with totemic symbols or crests. Displaying these hereditary crests and recounting the traditions of their acquisition formed an important part of potlatches. In the Wakashan area certain ceremonial cycles called for the dramatization of the whole tale of the supernatural encounter, which in some cases included the spirit-being's possession of and its eventual exorcism from the seeker; such dramas were performed by dancing societies.

A group of Tlingit dancers posing in front of totemic symbols, which also decorate their attire and drum (centre, front), *during a potlach ceremony in Haines, Alaska.* Marilyn Angel Wynn/Nativestock/Getty Images

Shamanism differed from other acquisitions of supernatural power only in the nature of the power obtained—that is, power to heal the sick through extraction of disease objects or recovery of a strayed soul. It was commonly believed that some shamans, or medicine men or women, had the power to cause infirmities as well as to cure them. Witchcraft was used to kill others or to make them ill and was believed to be carried out by malicious persons who knew secret rituals for that purpose.

PLATEAU INDIANS

Plateau religions shared several features with native North American religions in general. One was animism, the belief that spirits inhabited every person, animal, plant, and object. Another was the idea that individuals could communicate personally with the spirit world. A third was the belief that people called shamans gained supernatural powers through their contact with the spirits.

The main rituals were the vision quest; the firstling, or first foods, rites; and the winter dance. The vision quest was required for boys and recommended for girls. This rite of passage usually involved spending some days fasting on a mountaintop in hopes of communicating with a guardian spirit. The spirit was thought to guide the individual to a particular calling, such as hunting, warfare, or healing. Both boys and girls could become shamans, though it was seen as a more suitable occupation for males. Shamans cured diseases by extracting a bad spirit or an object that had entered the patient's body. On the northern Plateau they also brought back souls that had been stolen by the dead. Because their work included healing the living and contacting the dead, shamans tended to be both wealthy and respected—and even feared.

Firstling rites celebrated and honored the first foods that were caught or gathered in the spring. The first-salmon ceremony celebrated the arrival of the salmon run. The first fish caught was ritually sliced, and small pieces of it were distributed among the people and eaten. Then the carcass was returned to the water while people prayed and gave thanks. This ritual was believed to ensure

A tribal member overseeing the activity during a first-salmon ceremony. Alan Berner/Archive Photos/Getty Images

that the salmon would return and have a good run the next year. Some Salish had a "salmon chief" who organized the ritual. The Okanagan, Ntlakapamux, and Lillooet celebrated similar rites for the first berries rather than the first salmon.

The winter or spirit dance was a ceremonial meeting at which participants personified their respective guardian spirits. Among the Nez Percé the dramatic performances and the songs were thought to bring warm weather, plentiful game, and successful hunts.

CHAPTER 4

NATIVE AMERICAN SPIRIT BEINGS

Much like the ancient Greeks and Romans, Native American tribes have a slate of entities to whom they pay homage. Stories of how they came to be and whence their power sprang are shared from generation to generation, and many natural occurrences, human qualities, and various rites of passage are inextricably linked to their existence. Unlike the Greeks and Romans, however, these supernatural entities are not considered gods in the most common sense of the word. Instead, they are spirit beings that guide and influence humankind. Many of them live among people--not on high in a corollary to Mount Olympus--as embodied by anthropomorphized animals, including the many "tricksters" who work their magic on Earth.

Each Native American culture area—indeed, each tribe—has its own spirit beings, as well as a unique variation of overarching supernatural entities such as the Great Creator. The following offers a glimpse into the origin and activity of some of the most prevalent spirit beings know to a majority of tribes, as well as their place in Native American sacred life.

BEAR

B ear is a widespread culture hero and one of the most
powerful spirits in Native American religion wher-
ever actual bears live. Bear Man and Mother Bear myths
abound in North America. Courage, great strength,

*Kermode bears are referred to as spirit bears or ghost bears in some Native
American cultures. This specimen is with its black cub, eating barnacles in British
Columbia, Canada.* Daisy Gilardini/Photographer's Choice/Getty Images

wisdom, insight, and knowledge of the land are among qualities for which Bear is celebrated and respected. It has long been a totem figure.

A bear's ability to hibernate—a state of winter dormancy in which the body temperature is lowered and the creature sleeps in a state close to death—and awaken in the springtime makes it a symbol of rebirth. The female bear gives birth while in hibernation, and she is fiercely protective of her young for at least two years. Native American deeply respect this characteristic in particular.

According to one Bear Mother creation story, a young and disrespectful girl is lured away from her human family to marry a Bear, with whom she produces sons. When her brothers come to reclaim her, her Bear husband must die. He teaches her the proper way to hunt and to kill, and how to treat his corpse—information she, in turn, teaches her human clan. Her bear cubs, who are revealed to be human boys, become great hunters, and their offspring are the ancestors of modern humans. This story demonstrates several traits of Bear, including his association with the hunt, an activity he is said to protect and enable. It also reveals Bear's kinship with humans, a trait further seen in the ability to walk on its hind legs (bipedalism).

One subspecies of the American black bear held in high esteem is the kermode bear, which is found on islands along the coast of British Columbia and is the official animal of that Canadian province. Because a recessive gene causes about 1 in every 10 bears to be born with white fur, the kermode bear is known as the spirit bear or ghost bear. (Although it is sometimes considered an albino, many dark features, such as its nose, eyes, and paws contradict that categorization.) In Native American legend, the white color symbolizes snow and ice and is a reminder of the difficulties of the Ice Age.

The history of the Bear in human mythology stretches back many millennia. When such big game as the mammoth and the giant bison died out in the millennia before the Common Era, the bear survived, and with it the rituals surrounding its life and death. Ancient Slavs, Siberian peoples, and many northern Eurasian societies had bear cults. The event portrayed in the early-20th-century ballet *The Rite of Spring* by Igor Stravinsky bears witness to that association. Because experts believe that at least one stream of North American Indians migrated over the Bering Land Bridge, the likelihood of Bear's extremely ancient origins is strong.

BLUE JAY

Blue Jay is a trickster figure of the American Northwest. He is particularly present in the mythology of the Chinook Indians. Much like the familiar bird, Blue Jay is known for his noisiness, habit of gossiping, love of shiny objects, and stealing food. Blue Jay bears the bad characteristics that are typical of trickster figures. He exhibits greed, gluttony, and sexual excess, and is both cunning and foolish. Through his behaviour he points up human weaknesses and provides the opportunity for sacred laughter.

Among the Coeur d'Alene, Flathead, Kalispel, Sanpoil, Spokane, and other Interior Salish peoples, Blue Jay has a powerful ritual role during the winter Stomp Dance (or Jump Dance), a two- or three-day-long ceremony presenting the group's prayers and dreams for the future. Only those associated with the Blue Jay spirit are allowed to perform this dance.

The Blue Jay dance ritual is held from sunset to sunrise. Until the beginning of the ceremony, the dancer prepares himself by sleeping in a special lodge, blackening his face (and sometimes more of his body), and preparing himself physically for the dance. Once the midwinter ceremony begins, the dancer "becomes" Blue Jay. The dancer who is transformed into Blue Jay displays characteristic bird-like movements. He usually carries or wears identifying items, too. Flapping his "wings," he jumps or "flies" to the rafters of the lodge house and moves out into the night sky. When he reappears (and the dance is over), he retains his

The trickster Blue Jay is known for, among other traits, stealing food and gluttony. Frank Cezus/Photographer's Choice/Getty Images

transformational power—his Blue Jay-ness—and is not to be touched by other participants. While in this state, Blue Jay blesses the ritual food and also prophesies the future. He is ultimately captured by force and must undergo a ceremonial death. The human dancer must be smudged with cedar incense and revivified by the medicine man.

CORN
MOTHER

Indigenous agricultural tribes of North America believe that Corn Mother is responsible for the origin of corn (maize). Her story is related in two main versions, each of which has many variations. In all variants, the woman is responsible not only for the life-bringing food plant, but also for the rituals that should attend its planting and growth.

In the first main version, also called the "immolation version," the Corn Mother is depicted as an old woman who succors a hungry tribe, frequently adopting an orphan as a foster child. She secretly produces grains of corn by rubbing her body. When her secret is discovered, the people, disgusted by her means of producing the food, accuse her of witchcraft. Before being killed—by some accounts with her consent—she gives careful instructions on how to treat her corpse. Corn sprouts from the places over which her body is dragged or, by other accounts, from her corpse or burial site.

In the second version, or the "flight version," she is depicted as a young, beautiful woman who marries a man whose tribe is suffering from hunger. She secretly produces corn, also, in this version, by means that are considered to be disgusting. Discovered and insulted by her in-laws, she flees the tribe and returns to her divine home. Her husband follows her, and she gives him seed corn and detailed instructions for its cultivation.

American anthropologist Elsie Worthington Clews in her book *Pueblo Indian Religion* (1939) recorded the

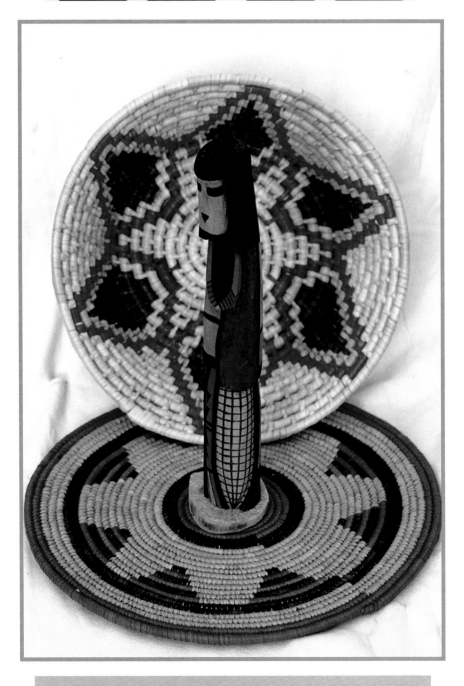

Example of a Zuni kachina doll depicting the Corn Mother. Marilyn Angel Wynn/Nativestock/Getty Images

presence of a number of corn fetishes used or given in relation to childbirth and naming rituals. An ear of corn is passed over the body of a woman in labour. The ear rests beside the infant after it is born and together with a second ear is wrapped and placed below the baby's cradle until the next planting season, when it is used as seed corn. Corn fetishes are also used in other ceremonies.

Both corn (in the form of ears, kernels, and pollen) and its originator, Corn Mother, were and remain significant to the Pueblo cultures of the southwest. Notably, similar Native American traditions of the immolation of a maternal figure or the insult to and flight of a beautiful maiden are told to account for the origin of the buffalo, peyote, certain medicinal herbs, and the sacred pipe.

COYOTE

One of the best-known trickster figures is Coyote, who is popular in the Northwest and the far West and on the plains of North America. In his trickster role, like others of his type, he plays tricks (sometimes at his own expense), targeting both humans and other animals. In general Coyote and other tricksters represent some of

Coyote has something of a dual personality. Some tribes emphasize his trickster qualities, such as stealing the Sun and creating winter. Others consider him a noble spirit. Greg Winston/National Geographic Image Collection/Getty Images

the worst traits of humankind—indulgence, greed, and the lack of self-restraint. In some stories he is selfish, greedy, or boasting. In other stories he is a noble figure, such as when he tricks the Frog People out of their exclusive control of water.

The last example shows Coyote as an animal culture hero, that is, a figure who is responsible for some act of great importance to humanity. Among some tribes, Coyote is considered responsible for such things as the origin of winter (by stealing light and allowing the Sun and Moon to escape Earth) and the introduction of death to humans (unless people died, he pointed out, too many would exist and there would be no room to grow corn). He also is said, for example, to have played a role in the creation of the world and of humans. The Nez Percé tell a story in which Coyote battles and kills a monster who has eaten many creatures. He then sprinkles water on the monster's bones, restoring life to those who were consumed, and distributes parts of the monster's body throughout North America to create various native groups.

In addition to his power as creator, or (sometimes) assistant to the Great Creator, Coyote is a shape-shifter and is able to transform himself into a human or other animal. Often, in the stories, he changes shape simply to have his way with some woman he desires. In whatever role, Coyote is a powerful figure and one of the most universal symbols among Native Americans.

DEER WOMAN

A number of Native Americans have stories about Deer Woman, a powerful, shape-shifting being who can appear as an old woman, a beautiful young woman, half-woman-half deer, or as a deer. She is associated with rituals of maturation, courtship, marriage, and fertility.

Stories about Deer Woman are widespread, from the Pacific Northwest and the Karuk of California, to the Cherokee, Seminole, Choctaw, and Muskogee, associated with the southeastern United States. One such tale comes from the Indians of the Southeast—Cherokee, Seminole, Choctaw, and Muskogee. In it a male dancer is taking a break from a powwow. He sees lights in a field and goes closer to investigate. It proves to be a beautiful woman dancing in the distance. Her clothing and gold headband catch the light. He is drawn to her brightly coloured clothes (or in some versions her nakedness) and thick lustrous braids. He follows her, getting closer, but never quite close enough to touch or embrace her. He notices the warm brown of her skin.

She lures him further and further from the stomp (dancing) grounds until he is in the dark forest and very near her. He makes the mistake of looking into her soft, large, brown eyes. She tantalizes him, luring him ever further into the woods. He can no longer see the lights of the gathering, and he barely hears its sounds. Still driven by his desire, he is nonetheless getting tired and he stumbles. Looking down he notices the tracks of deer hooves, and then he realizes whom he has been following. In some scenarios, the man is wounded by the hooves of the powerful shape-shifter (now in the form of a deer), and, far from the stomp ground, his family, and friends, he dies alone.

Native American writer Carolyn Dunn equates Deer Woman's cultural function in Indian society with those of the fairies in European cultures. Like the pixies, Deer Woman is intended to teach the lesson that if you stray too far from your community and its rules, you end up lost, or even dead.

GREAT CREATOR

The supreme being of all Native Americans goes by a number of names. The Zuni call this creator being Awonawilona ("the Maker and Container of All"). In the beginning the male-and-female dual creator Awonawilona existed alone in a black void. It created mist and steams, transforming itself into the Sun and causing the waters to condense and become an ocean. Awonawilona made the waters fruitful and matter grew on the waters. This material was split into Sky Father and Earth Mother, who produced all living beings.

The Algonquin and Ojibwa (Anishinaabe) know the Great Creator as Kitchi-Manitou ("Great Spirit"), but their creator differs from that of the Zuni in being neither male nor female. Kitchi-Manitou is also known as the Master of Life or the Sky Chief. The Great Spirit created water, earth, wind, and fire and then created human beings and sent them the culture hero Manabozho, to teach them.

Maheo ("Great One"), who is also called Great Medicine or Great Spirit, is the Cheyenne Great Creator. Like virtually all other Native American creator spirits, he has no form or attributes. He created Earth and all its creatures. He first created water and creatures of the water—fish, mussels, crawfish, and snails. In turn he made water birds and gave them sky to fly in and light to see by. And in time he appointed Grandmother Turtle to carry earth from the ocean bottom, to form dry ground. Then he made humans and land creatures and last of all, he made his most perfect creature, the buffalo.

Other Native American tribes have different names for the Great Creator. One of his most poetic names is that given to him by the Lakota: Wakan Tanka ("Great Mystery"). Usually in creation myths, the Great Creator departs after he has finished his work. He leaves the work of guiding humans and teaching them how to live to culture heroes and other spirit beings he has provided.

KOKOPELLI

Kokopelli, a dancing hunchbacked human flute player, may be the most recognizable figure of the Native Americans of the Southwest. He is depicted in petroglyphs and ancient pottery found throughout the Four Corners region—Utah, Colorado, New Mexico, and Arizona. His earliest representation was found on Hohokam culture pottery, and he was clearly a

Petroglyph of the popular trickster figure Kokopelli, etched on a rock in New Mexico's Galisteo Basin. Education Images/Universal Images Group/Getty Images

significant figure to the Ancient Pueblo peoples, who called him Anasazi.

Most of Kokopelli's physical characteristics have remained largely consistent. The items springing from his head—by turns a festive headdress, feathers, or light rays—are always present in an even number. They are sometimes considered antennae, as Kokopelli is occasionally associated with the grasshopper or katydid. One of his feet is on the ground, the other lifted in dance. His flute is always visible, held up to his mouth.

Kokopelli is most often seen in his trickster role, though he is not considered foolish, mischievous, or bad-natured, like many tricksters. As a dancer and musician he traveled to villages, spreading joy with his music and bringing fertility to the land—and to the people. From a great distance, he himself was said to have been able to impregnate girls bathing in a river. He was looked to for help when women could not get pregnant.

In his travels from village to village he carries a sack. The contents of the sack vary from group to group. Some say he carries seed corn for planting, others say gifts to accomplish his seductions, and still others say he carries seeds for all the plants of the world, which he spreads each spring, when he brings the rain.

MANABOZHO

Among the Indians of the Northeast—such as the Algonquin and Anishinaabe, or Ojibwa, people—Manabozho was an important culture hero. He also appears as a shape-shifting trickster and is one of very few such figures seen mostly in human form. Some tribes consider him a messenger of the Great Spirit.

The following story about the trickster Manabozho comes from the Menominee people of what is now Minnesota. In it Manabozho asks Buzzard for a ride on his back and asks him to be careful not to fly so wildly that his passenger falls off. At first things are fine. Manabozho gradually manages to look down and is amazed at the view. Buzzard cannot resist getting the better of him, however, and he banks suddenly, tipping Manabozho off and sending him plunging to Earth. He thinks Manabozho is dead and that he will return later to feast on him.

But Manabozho is only knocked out. When he recovers he vows revenge. Buzzard, who is getting hungry, spots a dead deer on the ground. He eyes it carefully to see if it's a trick, but the maggots on the body convince him that he has found an actual dead deer. He lands and digs his beak deep into the carrion. The disguised Manabozho grabs him around the throat and laughs. Buzzard finally manages to pull free, in the process losing all the feathers on his head and neck. Manabozho's trick is the reason that buzzards look so ugly to this day.

Manabozho's grandmother, Nokomis, raises Manabozho after the death of his mother in childbirth. Her name

Illustration from an early edition of Henry Wadsworth Longfellow's Song of Hiawatha, *showing Hiawatha* (a.k.a. Manabozho, left) *with his grandmother, Nokomis.* Culture Club/Hulton Archive/Getty Images

provides the clue to another of Manabozho's identities. Nokomis is the grandmother in poet Henry Wadsworth Longfellow's *Song of Hiawatha*; Longfellow called Manabozho Hiawatha.

RABBIT

Together with Coyote, Cottontail (Hare) is one of the main tricksters for the Native Americans living in the Southwest. He is also a significant figure for those in the Eastern Woodlands. He is known by various names, including White Hare, Great Hare, Jack Rabbit, and Lapin. The Algonquin know him as Mahtigwess (Mahtoqehs).

Brer Rabbit by Arthur Burdett Frost, who illustrated Joel Chandler Harris's Uncle Remus stories. The Bridgeman Art Library/Getty Images

Interestingly, as the trickster Rabbit (or Brer Rabbit), he is familiar to many from Joel Chandler Harris's Uncle Remus stories. Harris himself believed that the Brer Rabbit stories traveled to the "New World" with enslaved Africans, though modern scholars do not necessarily agree with this assertion. Some present-day scholars see the presence of Rabbit stories in both groups as "clear evidence of the intense interaction and cultural syncretism between Native American and African American cultures."

Whatever Cottontail's origins, he is known for a few traits: many of them have to do with his theft of food and water. He is also said to have killed the Sun, which was so hot that it caused the ground to boil. After killing it, Rabbit creates clouds, the stars, and the moon—and restores a less intense Sun to the sky. Among the legends of some tribes, Rabbit's magic powers are vast. The Algonquin tell a story about how he manages (by shifting shapes and creating illusions many times over again) to deceive Wild Cat (Lynx), who has sworn to kill him, and in the end Rabbit triumphs.

In another story, Rabbit starts a rumour that the Sun will disappear and frightens the other animals. He gets his long ears when the culture hero Gluzkap (First Man) pulls him by the ears from his hiding place. In yet another Rabbit loses his long tail but gains a wife. The Cherokee tell the story familiar to most Europeans and Euro-Americans through the fables of Aesop, in which Rabbit and Terrapin (Turtle) have a race. Rabbit is deceived when Terrapin's relatives (who look exactly like him) take turns appearing on the path ahead of him. Ultimately, he sees one of them cross the finish line ahead of him, and he never discovers that he has been tricked.

RAVEN

Raven predominates among the spirit beings of the Northwest Pacific Coast from Alaska to British Columbia. He bears great similarity to the figure of Coyote in the southwest, being at once trickster, culture hero, and creator. Like Coyote in his trickster aspect, Raven the trickster is driven by his desires, though Raven more often seeks food than sex.

The Raven cycle collects a group of traditional tales that feature Raven as an alternately clever and foolish bird-human whose voracious hunger, greed, and erotic appetite give rise to violent and amorous adventures that explain how the world of humans came to be.

Detail of a raven atop a Native American totem pole. Nancy Nehring/ iStock/Thinkstock

As in the trickster-transformer tales of other cultures, stories about Raven often begin with him instigating a crisis that precipitates social or physical chaos. The tales then recount the ultimate resolution of these crises (often at Raven's expense) and the re-establishment of order.

The Raven cycle begins with a boy's birth and relates early adventures that include his seduction of his aunt (or sometimes the daughter of the Sky Chief). Because he has transgressed incest (or status) rules, the boy subsequently flies to the sky to escape the flood that ensues. Raven, who is the product of this scandalous union, falls to earth during the flight. There Raven is adopted by a chief.

As an adult, Raven transforms the earth from a dark and arid land inhabited by a variety of ferocious monsters into a land of rivers, lakes, and mountains inhabited by animals and human beings. He travels about changing aspects of the physical environment into their present forms, often through deception.

The dozens of tales that recount his activities include Raven's impersonation of a woman to embarrass a man; his killing of a monster by putting hot stones down its throat; and his role as the "bungling host," a common motif of a guest who is fed by an animal wizard, then tries to imitate it in producing food but, lacking his host's magic, fails dismally.

SALMON

A figure that is particularly important to Native Americans of the Northwest Coast is Salmon. A story is told of four brothers who brought salmon to the Squamish people by negotiating with the Salmon People. In the end, the Salmon Chief agreed to send salmon in a particular order: Spring, Sockeye, Coho, Dog-Salmon, and Humpback. The Salmon Chief agreed to do this only

Tlingit rattle in the shape of a salmon. Inside the rattle is a carved figure of a shaman, solidifying Salmon's place in the spirit world. Werner Forman/Universal Images Group/Getty Images

if the tribes treated the fish with great respect, not wasting the flesh or taking more than they needed. Failure to behave respectfully always offended and angered the Salmon People and could result in sparse or no fish in the otherwise teeming streams.

The Salmon People appeared as humans, but they would be changed into fish when they walked into the water and the water reached their faces. That is, according to the stories, Salmon are supernatural beings who voluntarily assume fish form each year in order to sacrifice themselves for the benefit of humankind.

On being caught, these spirit-beings returned to their home beneath the sea, where they were reincarnated if their bones or offal were returned to the water. If not, as mentioned above, they would refuse to return to the river. As a result of their sensitivity, there were many specific prohibitions on acts believed to offend them and a number of observances designed to placate them. The most important of these was the first-salmon ceremony.

This rite varied in detail but invariably involved honouring the first salmon of the main fishing season by sprinkling them with eagle down, red ochre, or some other sacred substance, welcoming them in a formal speech, cooking them, and distributing their flesh, or morsels of it, communion-fashion, to all the members of the local group and any guests. The most comprehensive elaboration of this rite occurred in northwestern California in what have been called world-renewal ceremonies. These combined first-salmon rituals, first-fruits observances, and dances in which lineage wealth was displayed. Elsewhere the first-salmon rituals were less elaborate but still important.

SAYNDAY

S aynday, usually portrayed as a human (though he can change himself into animal form), is both trickster figure and culture hero. He is unique to the Kiowa people of Kansas, Oklahoma, and Texas, who migrated with a small band of Kiowa Apache from what is now southwestern Montana. Many stories are told about Saynday, both as a helper of the Kiowa and as a troublemaker. (His name, incidentally, is spelled many other ways, including Sendah, Sende, and Sainday.)

All stories of Saynday begin with the same formulaic sentence: "Saynday was coming along." According to the ethnologist Alice Lee Merriott, that introduction was one of three rules that Saynday established. The other two were that the tales should be told in winter, when work outside was finished, and they should also be told at night, when the day's work was done.

In one story, Saynday's world was constantly in darkness, which no one liked. With the help of Fox, Deer, and Magpie, Saynday contrived to gain possession of the Sun from the people who owned it. When he managed to capture it, the animals again grew unhappy, because plants grew too fast, the Sun was too bright outside, and it was never dark.

Saynday attempted to solve the problem by moving the Sun further away. For example, he put the Sun on top of a tipi, but it burned the tipi down. Finally, Saynday threw the Sun into the Sky, where it remained. That act proved to be the best solution after all, because that way the Sun could be shared with the people on the other side of the world, and everyone could have plenty of food and time to rest.

The Kiowa also say that Saynday played a role in the birth of the Kiowa people through a hollow cottonwood log. In other stories, Saynday brings the buffalo to his people, tries to marry Whirlwind and learns the hard way that he cannot, gets caught in a tree, runs a race with Coyote, and so on. There is also a grimmer story about Saynday meeting Smallpox, "the White Man's gift." In this story, Saynday protects his people by sending Smallpox to the much more numerous Pawnee.

SEDNA

Sedna, also called Sea Woman or She Who Does Not Want a Husband, is a powerful Inuit (Eskimo) sea goddess to the people of northern Canada and Greenland. She is the mother of all creatures and ruler of the underworld, called Adlivun.

Stories about Sedna begin differently, but they end the same way. In one version of her story, Sedna becomes so hungry for flesh that she begins to eat her own parents. They put out to sea with her in an *umiak* and when they have gone some distance, they shove her overboard.

Artist Joan Relke's bronze sculpture of Inuit spirit being Sedna, the powerful ruler of the underworld. Joan Relke http://sculptors.net.au

When she clings to the boat they cut off her fingers, which fall into the ocean and become sea creatures— whales, seals, and fish. When she can no longer hold on, she joins these creatures in the sea, and from that point on she rules over all creatures on land and sea and determines their movements.

In another version, which emphasizes her relationship to her father (Anguta), she is lured from her home to marry a man who proves to be a shape-shifting sea bird. She calls on her father to help her escape. In some versions she kills her husband and his death is avenged by other sea birds. In others she escapes with her father and her husband himself comes after her. Thinking to save himself when a storm arises, Anguta tosses his daughter over the side of his kayak. As she attempts to reboard, he cuts off her fingers and they become the creatures of the sea over which she has dominion.

Sedna is seen as the reason for sparse fishing and hunting. When that happens a shaman (a medicine person who can communicate with the spirit world) must journey to Adlivun to comb the human filth from Sedna's hair—having no fingers, she is unable to do it herself. Once that act has occurred, the natural balance is restored.

SKY WOMAN

Sky Woman (also called Woman-Who-Fell-From-The-Sky) is a figure in the creation myth of the Seneca people of what is now western New York state and eastern Ohio. (The Seneca were the largest of the original five nations of the Iroquois Confederacy.)

There are many versions of the creation story, but several details are present in all. Before people lived on Earth, they lived in the Sky World with the Sky Chief. Sky Woman, who is sometimes portrayed as the Sky Chief's pregnant wife and sometimes as his pregnant daughter, causes the uprooting of the World Tree—which is the source of food, light, and other good things. When the tree is down, Sky Woman goes to look at the hole caused by the uprooting and she falls into the hole. As she falls she grasps at plants and the tree roots to prevent herself from falling. She cannot stop herself, however, and soon she falls through the bottom of the Sky.

As she is falling, the animals of the water world below grow alarmed when they see that she will not be able to live in water as they do. They decide that Turtle will form the land that she can rest on, and they dive very deep to find soil. The mud on the floor of the ocean is so far from the surface of the water that many creatures lose their lives in the unsuccessful attempt to retrieve some dirt to cover Turtle's back. Finally one creature succeeds. Birds help Sky Woman to the newly created land, where she releases the seeds and roots she has grabbed in her fall. She also gives birth to a daughter who she teaches the ways of the world.

Sky Woman's daughter is impregnated by the West Wind, and, in giving birth to her twin sons, she dies. Sky Woman thus is grandmother and sole support for two boys who represent the opposing principles of good and evil, light and darkness.

SNAKE

I n general Native American people do not think well of snakes. Such types as horned snakes (such as Big Water Snake of the Blackfoot people), rattlesnakes, and feathered snakes (like Quetzalcóatl, the Feathered Serpent of ancient Mesoamerica) are well-known in indigenous legend. Snakes usually are considered powerful and violent. Certain tribes, however, consider them sacred.

A pictograph of a snake figuring prominently among drawings—which also include a bird and shamans—on a clay wall of a Shawnee building. Nativestock.com/Marilyn Angel Wynn/Getty Images

Southeastern tribes, notably the Creek and Natchez, tell a story about a Tie-Snake society and its king that illustrates why they consider Tie-Snake a protector being. (Tie-Snakes, by the way, look just like typical snakes—no horns or feathers—but they have extraordinary strength and can wrap around humans.)

In this story (one of many about Tie-Snakes), a young boy is sent by his father, a chief, on a mission to another chief. He is to show a certain pot to the other chief as a sign of his authority. The boy interrupts his journey to play with some boys he meets by a river, and in the process—thinking the pot will float—he throws the pot into the river and it sinks. He knows he cannot return to his father and report that he has lost the pot, so he jumps into the river to attempt to retrieve it. When he dives below the surface, Tie-Snakes grab the boy and take him to their king.

In the presence of the king the boy has his resolve tested and each time on his fourth attempt to accomplish some task, he succeeds. The King of the Tie-Snakes admires and likes the boy, presents him with two gifts—a feather and a tomahawk—and restores to him his father's pot. After three days the boy is allowed to return to his people. Before sending him home, the King of the Tie-Snakes tells the boy how to summon him if his father needs help against enemies.

When the time comes to request the Tie-Snakes' aid, the boy takes his tomahawk and wears his feather to ask the King of the Tie-Snakes for aid. Help is provided— Tie-Snakes restrict the movement of the other tribe—and the boy's father not only triumphs over his enemies but makes peace with them.

SPIDER

A significant figure of the Great Plains is Spider, whose stories vary according to the culture being examined. Among Spider's many roles are those of trickster, culture hero, and sometimes even creator.

Among the Hopi, Spider is known as Grandmother Spider (also called Spider Old Woman). She is seen as the assistant to the Great Creator in charge of the world we know. By mixing earth and saliva, she created the Twin Gods who helped bring form and order to the pre-human

A Navajo weaver working at her craft. In Navajo culture, Spider is credited with teaching humans to weave, much as spiders spin or "weave" their webs.
David Edwards/National Geographic Image Collection/Getty Images

Earth. She later formed humans to inhabit the world she helped create.

The Navajo know her as Spider Woman. Although she is not a creator among the Navajo, she is an important culture hero. She is credited with having taught the Navajo agriculture and, not surprisingly for an arachnid, the art of weaving, which was and remains a signature skill among the Navajo. The Choctaw and Cherokee say that Spider Woman taught them the art of pottery-making.

The Spider figure is often associated with the gift of fire. In one story, the Thunder Spirits cause a fire to burn on an island. Grandmother Spider is the only creature who can both get to the island and return with an ember. She spins a thread that she rides to the island. When there she weaves a basket (or makes a small pot) in which she can carry a coal back to the other animals. In one version of this story, the animals decide that fire is too dangerous, so they give it to humans.

Spider Man, on the other hand, is not portrayed as simply helpful or benevolent, as Spider Woman usually is. He is a complicated trickster figure, both powerful and untrustworthy. The Lakota and some others call him Iktomi. He can be spider-sized or human-sized. Sioux legends usually speak of him as a human, though even in human form he retains all of the boastfulness, egoism, and inappropriate behaviours typical of tricksters. He is considered very smart, but often in trying to trick others he ends up hurting himself.

According to the Dakota Sioux ethnographer Ella Deloria (whose book *Dakota Texts* translates a number of popular tales of Iktomi), "the sentence 'He is playing Iktomi' is understood to mean that a person is posing as a very agreeable fellow, simply to get what he wants."

THUNDERBIRD

Thunderbird is another widespread figure in Native American legend. He is present in the legends as a powerful spirit who personifies natural energy. The most iconic description of him is that of a huge hawk-like bird who carries the rain on his back, whose enormous flapping wings produce the sound of thunder and blinking eyes and whose opening and closing beak (and sometimes eyes) produce flashes of lightning. He is typically depicted in art in a proud stance with his legs and wings spread.

In the Pacific Northwest, Thunderbird was thought to be able to hold whales in his talons and to fly with his prey into the mountains. In *Kutenai Tales*, anthropologist Franz Boas recorded several Kutenai legends concerning the Thunderbird. In some of these, Thunderbird is tricked and killed, but even without his spirit his feathers have the power to help his killers to fly.

To the Lakota, who call Thunderbird Wakinyan, he is but one of the mighty Thunder Beings whose return heralds the spring. He is seen as both creative and destructive, bringing the rains that help crops grow and yet causing damaging winds, occasional floods, and fires.

One of the more interesting beliefs of the Lakota, as detailed in books such as James R. Walker's *Lakota Belief and Ritual* is the association of Thunderbird with the person of the *heyoka* (sacred clown). When Thunderbird (or any Thunder Being) appeared in a person's dreams, that person was required to participate in a *heyoka* ceremony, to become a *heyoka*.

A Plains Indian ghost dance shirt featuring a thunderbird, striking the spirit being's traditional pose with legs extended and wings spread. Werner Forman/Universal Images Group/Getty Images

The ceremony itself is described in great detail in *Black Elk Speaks*, as told to John G. Neihardt. The *heyoka* connection to Thunderbird imparted great power to the *heyoka*, who was considered his human hands. The role of heyoka lasted a lifetime and entailed great responsibility. It required fortitude, compassion, and healing powers. Anyone who refused to undergo the ceremony and take on the role was believed to risk being killed by lightning. Perhaps the best-known *heyoka* was the Oglala Sioux chief Crazy Horse.

TWIN
BROTHERS

Twins are a motif that is common to many cultures of the world—including those of Native American tribes. Sometimes the twins are presented simply as cooperative siblings and heroes, and in other stories they are opposites, one good and the other evil.

The Caddo people, once native to Louisiana and Arkansas, but now largely in Oklahoma, have a good story about twin brothers who grow up separately. The story begins with Medicine Man and Clay Pot Woman, who fall in love and marry and make a home on the riverbank outside of their village.

Clay Pot Woman becomes pregnant and under difficult circumstances bears a male child, but in the usual way. When Medicine Man cleans up and takes to the midden heap (garbage pile) the herbs and charms he has provided to help his wife and the soiled materials from the birth, a second son is born there (in the midden heap) by magic. The second twin makes his way into the forest to live there, with the aid of supernatural beings and animal companions.

A human-eating ogre captures Clay Pot Woman as she goes to fetch water from the river. Father and son mourn her death. While Medicine Man carries on with his usual activities, the brothers meet up and become fast companions. Eventually the forest-raised twin joins his father and brother.

One day the growing boys set off together to gain their manhood names. They are tested and reborn. One becomes Lightning and the other Thunder. They find their mother's bones, reconstitute her body, and slay the Ogre Chief. The family of four is reunited, and they live well until Medicine Man and Clay Pot Woman die. The sons bury them. No longer wishing to be on earth, the brothers go off to live in the sky, where they make their presence known in wind and bad weather.

In addition to the style of story exemplified here, Native American legends speak of Warrior Twins (sons of the Sun, who rid the human world of monsters) and numerous versions of twins who oppose each other and counteract each other's powers. The Yuma twins Kokomaht and Bakotahl are one of many examples of the latter type.

WHITE BUFFALO CALF WOMAN

Another of the significant supernatural beings of the Lakota was called White Buffalo Calf Woman. She is considered a sort of saviour of the Lakota people, who taught them many important life lessons and showed them how to live correctly. A brief summary of the essential story follows.

Two hunters spot White Buffalo Calf Woman (wearing white buckskin) in the distance, and, seeing that she is

One traditional story tells how the shape-shifting White Buffalo Calf Woman got her name by appearing to hunters as a white buffalo calf on a cloud. Valerie Shaff/Iconica/Getty Images

beautiful, one of them—despite the warnings of his friend—goes to embrace her. As he does so, he collapses into a pile of bones on the ground. White Buffalo Calf Woman tells the other hunter that he should return to his people and tell them of her impending visit.

The second hunter returns home alone and announces that they will have a visitor and should prepare a feast. Four days after the fateful meeting, a cloud appears in the sky, bearing a white buffalo calf. The creature shifts its shape and becomes White Buffalo Calf Woman.

She holds in her hands a sacred, or medicine, bundle (a wrapped package seldom opened that contains certain sacred objects). She opens the bundle to reveal the objects treasured by the Lakota, including a sacred pipe, whose elements symbolize the plants and creatures of the earth and sky.

White Buffalo Calf Woman shows the people how the sacred pipe should be smoked. She also urges them to observe the seven sacred ceremonies, including the Sweat Lodge (a means of purification), Sun Dance (oldest of the sacred ceremonies), and the Vision Quest (a four-day fast held in search of a revelatory vision). After White Buffalo Calf Woman has given the medicine bundle and imparted the information about the sacred ceremonies, she changes once again into a buffalo and disappears, with a vow to return again.

WHITE-PAINTED WOMAN

White-Painted Woman is a major figure in the religion of the Apache people of the southwest. (She is a counterpart to the Navajo's Changing Woman.) Each Apache band (subgroup) has its own version of stories about her. She is said to have existed at the beginning of time. In one story the Creator warns her about the coming of a Great Flood, and she saves herself by floating in a shell on the floodwaters until they abate.

White-Painted Woman is the mother of two culture heroes, Killer-of-Enemies and Child of the Water. (In some versions of the story, she is the mother of only Killer-of-Enemies, and White Shell Woman bears Child-of-the-Water.) The stories of these two offspring share many themes with the Twin Brothers or Warrior Twins.

Many Apache ceremonies originated with White-Painted Woman, including the female puberty rites. In this rite, she promises the adolescent long life and good fortune in return for rituals correctly performed. The maiden ceremony, as it is sometimes called, is a four-day social event—to reflect both the number of days of creation and the four stages of a woman's life (girl, young woman, middle age, old age)—involving feasts and dancing as well as religious activities. Two figures, a shaman (who may be female) and a woman attendant, direct the events, and masked dancers perform. The shaman builds a ceremonial tipi according to certain principles. While doing so, he or she sings a particular song.

Meanwhile, the woman attendant ritually dresses the girl in a special order from foot to head. The woman further advises her on such matters as her ritual responsibilities and the appropriate demeanour. The girl enters the tent and is painted with pollen, a substance sacred to the Apache. She then paints her attendant with pollen too. The girl is also painted with red clay and white clay. She does not wash until the end of the ceremony.

An Apache girl (left) stands with her attendant during the young maiden's coming-of-age ceremony, in 1955. The ceremony is associated with the spirit being White-Painted Woman. © AP Images

A first-morning ritual involves the girl running four times around a basket filled with the ritual tools and materials. After she return to the tent the last time, she distributes presents of food and tobacco. The girl spends the remainder of the day quietly indoors, while celebrants visit, play games, and make preparations outdoors.

In the first-evening ceremony a large fire is lit in the ceremonial tent, and the masked dancers perform several types of dances. After a time, the girl is led to the tent. A singer sings prescribed songs, and the girl herself dances prescribed dances. This activity continues late into the night.

Except for the morning ritual, the next three days are similar. At sunrise on the fifth day of the ceremony, the shaman or medicine man paints an image of the Sun on his palm, by this means bringing the Sun to Earth. He imparts the power of the Sun to the girl by rubbing its painted image on the girl's head and face. The adolescent is referred to as the White-Painted Woman's sister, and she wears her ceremonial garb for four days after the ceremony.

WOLVERINE

Stories of the trickster figure Wolverine are widespread. The Innu (Montagnais and Naskapi) people of what is now northeastern Canada consider Wolverine (whom they call Kuekuatsheu) a creator figure. Although he is considered a trickster, he is not as greedy or violent as many of the others are. He saves other animals in a large boat, like Noah's Ark. After the Great Flood, he creates land with the help of Muskrat or Mink. One or the other of these companion figures dives down to the ocean floor to recover some mud and rocks. Wolverine uses these materials to create the world.

The Malicite (Maliseet), Mi'kmaq, and Passamaquoddy peoples know Wolverine as Lox, or Master Lox. The Mi'kmaq also call him Keekwajoo. This figure is not as benign as Kuekuatsheu. In one story, for example, Master Lox tells a number of ducks and geese that he is going to give a powwow and invites them all to his tipi. There he tells them they must shut their eyes as he talks, or they will be blind. While their eyes are closed, he kills them one by one, until finally one of them opens an eye, sees what is going on, and sounds the alarm.

Another story of the Ojibwa, Cheyenne, and Lakota reveals how easy it is to trick Wolverine. Two foolish girls, fantasizing about sleeping with stars, are taken by the Star People to have their wishes fulfilled. They live with the Star People far from home for a long time and wish to return to their people. When they make a rope to lower themselves down to Earth again, they land in an eagle's nest and are stuck there. They try to interest

Wolverine is a trickster, but some Native American cultures credit him with saving the world's animals from a flood and rebuilding Earth.
Thomas Kitchin & Victoria Hurst/All Canada Photos/Getty Images

various creatures in helping them down, but Bear and Lynx refuse them.

Finally they see Wolverine, who is poor and very ugly, and tell him they will marry him if he helps them. Removing their hairpins and putting them in the nest, they are rescued by Wolverine. He is very pleased with his new wives and shows them off to increase his prestige. One of them "suddenly" remembers that she left behind her hairpin. When Wolverine goes back to the eagle's nest to find the hairpins, his wives conspire with the trees in the forest to hide them when he returns. He never finds them, though he is always looking.

GLOSSARY

anachronism A person or a thing that seems to belong to the past and not to fit in the present.

animism The belief that all things—animate or otherwise—have a living essence and are capable of either helping or harming human beings.

anthropomorphize To attribute human form or personality to things not human.

cosmogony A theory of the origin of the universe.

culture area The anthropological term for a geographic region in which the inhabitants share many societal traits.

culture hero A figure who is responsible for some act of great importance to humanity.

deity One who has the rank or essential nature of a god.

demiurge One that is an autonomous creative force or decisive power.

dualism A theory that considers reality to consist of two irreducible elements or modes, typically good and evil.

embody To give a body to a spirit.

fetish An object that is believed to have magical powers.

imbue To permeate or influence as if by dyeing.

indigenous Having originated in, or being the first to occupy, a particular area or region.

personify To think of or represent something or an idea as a person or as having human qualities or powers.

petroglyph A carving or inscription on a rock.

phenomenon A rare or significant, observable fact or event.

polytheistic The belief in or worship of more than one god or supernatural being.

profane To treat something sacred with abuse, irreverence, or contempt.

ritual An act done according to religious law or in accordance with social custom.

shaman A man or woman who has shown an exceptionally strong affinity with the spirit world; also considered healers who are thought to be adept at divination.

totality The whole or entire amount.

trickster A cunning or deceptive character appearing in various forms in the folklore of many cultures

vision quest A supernatural experience in which an individual seeks to interact with a guardian spirit, usually an anthropomorphized animal, to obtain advice or protection.

FOR FURTHER READING

Bastian, Dawn E., and Judy K. Mitchell. *Handbook of Native American Mythology.* New York, NY: Oxford University Press, 2008.

Brown, Joseph. *Teaching Spirits: Understanding Native American Religious Traditions.* New York, NY: Oxford University Press, 2010.

Clark, Ella E., and Margot Edmonds. *Voices in the Winds: Native American Legends.* New York, NY: Castle Books, 2009.

Hartz, Paula R. *Native American Religions.* New York, NY: Chelsea House Publications, 2009.

Hill, Rick, and Teri Frazier. *Indian Nations of North America.* Des Moines, IA: National Geographic, 2010.

Jones, David M., and Brian L Molyneaux. *Mythology of the American Nations.* London, Eng.: Southwater Publishing, 2013.

Lankford, George E., ed. *Native American Legends of the Southeast: Tales from the Natchez, Caddo, Biloxi, Chicksaw, and Other Nations.* Tuscaloosa, AL: University of Alabama Press, 2011.

Lowenstein, Tom. *Native American Myths and Beliefs.* New York, NY: Rosen Publishing, 2012.

Lynch, Patricia Ann, and Jeremy Roberts. *Native American Mythology A to Z.* New York, NY: Chelsea House Publications, 2010.

Orr, Emma Restall. *The Wakeful World: Animism, Mind and the Self in Nature.* Alrestford, UK: Moon Books, 2012.

Pearce, Q.L. *Native American Mythology.* Farmington Hills, MI: Lucent Books, 2012.

Williams, Mike. *The Shaman's Spirit: Discovering the Wisdom of Nature, Power Animals, Sacred Places and Rituals.* London, Eng.: Watkins Publishing, 2013.

Zimmerman, Larry J. *Exploring the Life, Myth, and Art of Native Americans.* New York, NY: Rosen Publishing, 2010.

INDEX